D1092802

Graphic Medieval History

CASTLES

By Gary Jeffrey & Illustrated by Nick Spender

FRANKLIN WATTS

LONDON•SYDNEY

Franklin Watts
First published in Great Britain in 2018 by
The Watts Publishing Group

Designed by Gary Jeffrey and illustrated by Nick Spender

HB ISBN 978 1 4451 6723 7
PB ISBN 978 1 4451 6724 4

Printed in Malaysia

Franklin Watts
An imprint of
Hachette Children's Group
Part of The Watts Publishing Group
Carmelite House
50 Victoria Embankment
London EC4Y 0DZ

An Hachette UK Company
www.hachette.co.uk

www.franklinwatts.co.uk

GRAPHIC MEDIEVAL HISTORY CASTLES
was produced for Franklin Watts by
David West ⚇Children's Books, 11 Glebe Road, London SW13 0DR

Photo credits:
p5m, David Dixon, p5b, Jonaslange; p6, ChrisO; p7m, Clem Rutter,
p7b, derek billings; p44m, Humphrey Bolton; p45t, Jerzy Strzelecki,
p45m, Michael Hanselmann, p45b, PHGCOM; p46, Tequask; p47,
Antony McCallumi

Contents

Castle Building

Military forts and walled towns had existed since ancient times but private fortified strongholds only emerged in the 9th century, when the vast Frankish Empire split up into smaller territories, such as lordships and principalities.

MOTTE AND BAILEY

The early castle builders of France started by building a raised mound of earth, or motte. Next to the motte a fortified enclosure, or bailey, with outbuildings was laid. The top of the motte was fenced with timber and a timber guardhouse, or residence, was built in the centre. The whole castle complex would be surrounded by a ditch. The castle was an effective refuge against attack and a garrison for a small force that could control a large area. However motte and baileys were prone to rot and catch fire.

MEDIEVAL CASTLES
1. Bamburgh
2. Caernarfon
3. Carcassonne
4. Château-Gaillard
5. Conwy
6. Dover
7. Kenilworth
8. Llawharden
9. Lincoln
10. Malbork
11. Rochester
12. Tower of London
13. Warwick
14. Windsor

The massive Norman keep at the Tower of London was William the Conqueror's stronghold in the capital.

CASTLE KEEP

The Normans built their castles all over Britain from 1066, and rebuilt the most important ones in stone. The main fortress, or donjon, was called a keep and could have massively thick walls. Generally though an 11th-century castle only needed to be strong enough to hold off a besieging army until relief could arrive.

A 13th-century drawing of Lincoln Castle's hollow keep.

4

CRUSADER CASTLES

The crusades (1099–1272) created the European Crusader States in the Holy Land and caused the building of new, amazingly strong castles. They had towering concentric walls with projecting towers that gave good range to defensive archers. Only kings or the rich military orders could afford them.

Krak des Chevaliers in Syria was built by the wealthy Knights Hospitaller in 1170. It had concentric lines of defence (walls within walls).

A fortified wall of Carcassonne in France shows the timber galleries, or machicolations, that were built on most medieval castles.

Conwy Castle in Wales, in the UK, has a fortified gateway or 'barbican' protecting its west front.

GREAT CASTLES

The High Middle Ages was a tumultuous time in England and France and the peak of great castle building. Features such as battlements (a gapped parapet), barbicans, arrow slits, murder holes (ambush openings), and machicolations (drop openings over a wall) all appeared on castles in the 12th and 13th centuries. Castles like English King Henry II's great fortress at Dover (see page 20) could make a real difference to the future fate of a nation. The Welsh castles of Edward I (see page 36), enabled a king to become a conqueror.

Under Siege!

A hostile foreign force has invaded. The nobles and their army retreat to the safety of a castle. The invaders arrive and set up camp, and then begin the slow and dangerous process of trying to break into the fortress.

A 15th-century painting of a castle siege shows scaling ladders and a large defending army.

A perrier siege engine

CASTLE ATTACK

Siege towers

The besiegers build 'engines' out of wood that hurl large rocks against the castle walls. They erect towers as firing platforms that can also be pushed against the parapets so that troops can storm the top of the walls. Sappers dig at the foundations to undermine and topple stone towers. Heavy battering rams are forced against weak points and flaming arrows are fired into wooden structures on, or inside, the castle. If this fails, they hope to starve the defenders out before relief arrives.

A shielded ram

Undermining

CASTLE DEFENCE

Apart from the castle's design, the defenders have fewer options. The crossbow is an accurate long range weapon when fired through arrow slits. Boiling oil can be poured through machicolations on to attackers. A well-stocked castle with its own well can last out for months.

Château Gaillard was a strong, highly advanced English castle built in 1196 to defend Normandy, which at that time was a duchy of the English Crown. (See page 8.)

GREAT CASTLE SIEGES

In 1215 rebellious barons challenged the authority of England's King John and took control of Rochester Castle. John himself laid siege to the fortress and after catapults failed, he undermined the walls. The barons and their men retreated to the massive Norman stone keep while John sent men to dig beneath

The strategically important site of Rochester Castle in Kent, England, was besieged three times between 1088 and 1264. The last siege was relieved by Prince Edward (later King Edward I).

a corner tower. They lit pig fat to burn the mine props away, and toppled it. The barons retreated further behind a strong inner wall, still occupying half the building, but after a few weeks they were starved out – proof that even the strongest castle could be taken eventually.

The longest siege in medieval England took place 60 years later when forces loyal to Henry III attacked a group of defiant barons holed up in Kenilworth Castle, in Warwickshire, England. Deadly missiles were hurled at the walls but a flooded three-sided moat kept the attackers

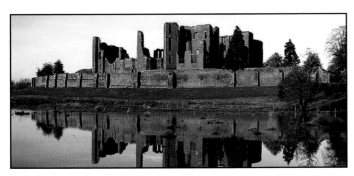

out until, six months later, the defenders ran out of food.

The imposing ruins of Kenilworth Castle, which resisted an epic siege in 1266, during a period of English civil war.

The Breaking of Château Gaillard

LATE SEPTEMBER 1203, ANGLO-NORMANS UNDER THE COMMAND OF ENGLISH KNIGHT, ROGER DE LACEY, WERE BESIEGED IN THEIR CASTLE AT CHÂTEAU GAILLARD, IN EAST NORMANDY, BY THE FORCES OF FRENCH KING PHILIP II.

GAILLARD WAS THE LAST OBSTACLE IN THE CONQUERING OF ALL OF NORMANDY.

HIS SIEGE ENGINES WERE READY.

AT LAST WE WILL DESTROY LIONHEART'S STRONGHOLD!*

*RICHARD I HAD BUILT GAILLARD.

THE STONE SMASHED THROUGH THE TIMBER MACHICOLATION, STOPPING THE DEFENDERS' FIRE.

KROOM

FRENCHMEN RAN FORWARDS WITH SCALING LADDERS.

ALLEZ! ALLEZ!

THE SIEGE TOWER WAS HURRIEDLY PUSHED INTO PLACE AS SCORES OF FRENCH SOLDIERS RUSHED THE RAMPARTS.

THE DEFENDERS FIRED THE WOODEN BUILDINGS AND RETREATED TO THE MIDDLE BAILEY.

BOLT THE GATE! BOLT THE GATE!

PHILIP REPOSITIONED HIS SIEGE ENGINES AND BEGAN THE TASK OF WRECKING THE MIDDLE BAILEY.

SIRE, I BEG YOUR PARDON, BUT THIS MAN SAYS HE HAS SOME IMPORTANT INFORMATION!

THE INFANTRYMAN'S NAME WAS BOGGIS.

SIRE, I HAVE SURVEYED ALL ROUND THE CASTLE AND I THINK I'VE FOUND SOMETHING...

...A WEAK SPOT.

BOGGIS LED THE KING ROUND TO THE OPPOSITE SIDE OF THE FORTRESS.

THESE ARE THE EXITS FOR THE GARDEROBES IN THE CURTAIN WALL.

FOR SOME REASON THEY MADE THEM QUITE LOW AND THEY'RE UNPROTECTED.

THE DROP BELOW IS STEEP BUT WITH OUR LADDERS, I THINK WE COULD REACH THEM...

LATER, IN THE DEAD OF NIGHT, BOGGIS EMERGED IN A CASTLE CLOSET.

THE REST OF HIS MEN FOLLOWED HIM.

UGH! IT STINKS!

SHSSSSSSH!

NOW WHAT?

MAKE AS MUCH NOISE AS YOU CAN!

THE PLAN WORKED. THE ANGLO-NORMANS BELIEVED THEY WERE BEING OVERRUN, SET FIRE TO THE WOODEN BUILDINGS AND FLED TO THE INNER BAILEY.

PUNGENT BUT TRIUMPHANT, BOGGIS LET THE ROYAL ARMY IN THROUGH THE MIDDLE BAILEY GATE.

THE DEFENDERS WERE NOW IN TROUBLE. THEY HAD LOST THEIR SUPPLIES AND, UNDER COVER OF THE FIXED DRAWBRIDGE, FRENCH SAPPERS BEGAN UNDERMINING THE INNER BAILEY WALLS...

IT'S NO GOOD - WE CAN'T GET AT THEM!

...BRINGING THE TOWERS EITHER SIDE CRASHING DOWN.

DE LACEY DECIDED THAT HIDING OUT IN THE KEEP WOULD BE POINTLESS AND SURRENDERED, AS PHILIP II'S STANDARD WAS RAISED OVER CHÂTEAU GAILLARD.

HIS WAY WAS NOW OPEN TO TAKE BACK NORMANDY FROM KING JOHN.

THE END

The Siege of Dover Castle

INVITED BY ENGLISH REBEL BARONS KEEN TO DEPOSE HATED KING JOHN, THE FRENCH PRINCE, LOUIS CAPET, HAD BEEN IN ENGLAND THREE MONTHS. ALREADY HE HAD CONQUERED HALF OF THE KINGDOM BUT THIS WOULD COUNT FOR NOTHING IF HE DIDN'T POSSESS MIGHTY DOVER CASTLE - THE 'KEY TO ENGLAND'.

THE SIEGE BEGAN ON 19TH JULY 1216, WITH AN ATTACK ON THE BARBICAN PROTECTING THE CASTLE GATE.

USING A COVERED WALKWAY TO STRADDLE THE OUTER DITCH, SAPPERS WORKED TO UNDERMINE THE TIMBER PALISADE WALLS.

A TUNNEL WAS DUG FORWARDS AND ANOTHER WALKWAY WAS PLACED AT THE BASE OF THE EASTERN GATEWAY TOWER. HERE THE CHALK GROUND CAME AWAY EASILY, EXPOSING MASSIVE TIMBER FOOTINGS.

CRUNCH

SMOOTH IT ON NICE AND THICK BOYS!

ANIMAL FAT WAS SPREAD ON THE TIMBERS, AND BUNDLES OF FAGGOTS AND DRIED GRASS WAS JAMMED INTO ANY GAPS.

A BRAVE VOLUNTEER THREW IN GRENADES OF GREEK FIRE* AND QUICKLY BACKED AWAY.

PLOOF!

THE INCANDESCENT MATERIAL EXPLODED THE TIMBERS INTO FLAME.

GO! GO! GO!

BALOOMPH!

*INFLAMMABLE CHEMICALS

WHEN ENOUGH TIMBER HAD BURNT AWAY, THE TOWER FELL.

KLUMPH

FRENCH SOLDIERS POURED INTO THE GAP.

ROAAAAR

ENGLISH KNIGHTS HACKED DESPERATELY TO STOP THE ONRUSHING HORDE WHILE GARRISON COMMANDER, HUBERT DE BURGH, ORDERED A RETREAT.

BACK! BACK TO THE TOWER!

CROSSBOWMEN MASSED ALONG THE TOWER TOPS OF THE MIDDLE BAILEY...

THEY UNLEASHED A HAIL OF DEADLY BOLTS ON THE INVADERS.

FLINK!

THE BRAVE FRENCH KEPT TRYING UNTIL...

THIS IS *MURDEROUS!* FALL BACK! FALL BACK!

IN THE LULL, DE BURGH ORDERED THE TIMBERS TO BE STRIPPED FROM THE COURTYARD BUILDINGS...

JUST THE CROSSBEAMS WILL DO - COME ON, HURRY!

CLUNK
CLUNK

... AND JAMMED TIGHTLY IN THE HOLE.

IT WAS A STAND OFF...

OUR MEN ARE EXHAUSTED. OFFER THE ENGLISH A TRUCE.

KING JOHN, FIGHTING IN LINCOLNSHIRE, WAS WEAK WITH SICKNESS WHEN HE HEARD THE NEWS.

GROAN! A TRUCE? HOW DARE THEY MAKE DEALS BEHIND MY BACK?

SEVEN DAYS LATER HE WAS DEAD.

LOUIS CALLED A CONFERENCE AND OFFERED DE BURGH A GREAT AMOUNT OF LAND AND POWER IF HE WOULD SURRENDER AND SERVE UNDER HIM.

HE SAYS HE MUST REFUSE OR HIS GARRISON WILL BE CALLED TREACHEROUS FOR GIVING UP.

LOUIS WENT BACK TO FRANCE BUT VOWED TO RETURN.

ON 13TH APRIL 1217 HE DID RETURN, WITH A FLEET AND A FRIGHTENING NEW WEAPON UNKNOWN IN ENGLAND – A GIANT, COUNTERWEIGHT-DRIVEN PERRIER, OR TREBUCHET.

AS THE FRENCH APPROACHED, FORCES LOYAL TO THE NEW KING, HENRY III, ATTACKED THEIR SIEGE CAMP ON DOVER CLIFFS.

WEEEHEEEHEE

THAK!

LOUIS AND HIS FLEET WERE FORCED TO LAND AT SANDWICH.

LOOSE!

THE MASSIVE COUNTERWEIGHT DROPPED, WHIPPING THE LONG ARM AROUND WITH GATHERING SPEED.

CREEEAAAAK

AT THE TOP OF ITS ARC, THE SLING LOOSED A HUGE GRANITE ROCK AT INCREDIBLE VELOCITY...

PHWUFFF

...STRAIGHT AT THE WALLS OF DOVER CASTLE.

THE ROCK EXPLODED WITH A REVERBERATING CRACK ON THE WALLS OF THE INNER BAILEY, SHOWERING DEBRIS ON THE MEN IN THE BARBICAN BELOW..

KRACK

BUT THE THICK WALL WAS NOT EVEN DENTED.

HURRAH!

IT LOOKED AS IF THE CASTLE MIGHT HOLD.

WHILE LOUIS VAINLY ATTEMPTED TO BREACH DOVER CASTLE, DISASTER STRUCK AT LINCOLN, WHERE ENGLISH SOLDIERS LAUNCHED A SUPRISE ATTACK ON THE FRENCH, BESIEGING ITS CASTLE AND COMPLETELY DEFEATING THEM.

LINCOLN

EAST ANGLIA

LOUIS'S LAST HOPE WAS REINFORCEMENTS THAT WERE COMING FROM FRANCE. MEANWHILE, HIS ENEMY FROM DOVER, HUBERT DE BURGH, WAS LEADING AN ENGLISH FLEET OUT TOWARDS THEM.

SIGNAL TO ENGAGE THE ENEMY!

THE FRENCH FLAGSHIP, CARRYING A TREBUCHET, WAS SURROUNDED BY ENGLISH SHIPS AND PELTED WITH BAGS OF QUICKLIME, BLINDING ITS CREW.

BOUFF!

BOUFF!

THE CAPTURED FRENCH CAPTAIN, A NOTORIOUS PIRATE, WAS GIVEN A CHOICE.

YOU CAN EITHER BE LAUNCHED FROM THAT THING, OR BEHEADED AT THE RAIL!

FLENCH

34

LOUIS GAVE UP HIS ATTEMPT TO WIN THE THRONE OF ENGLAND. THE STRENGTH OF DOVER CASTLE HAD EFFECTIVELY SAVED THE KINGDOM.

THE END

Edward I Conquers Wales

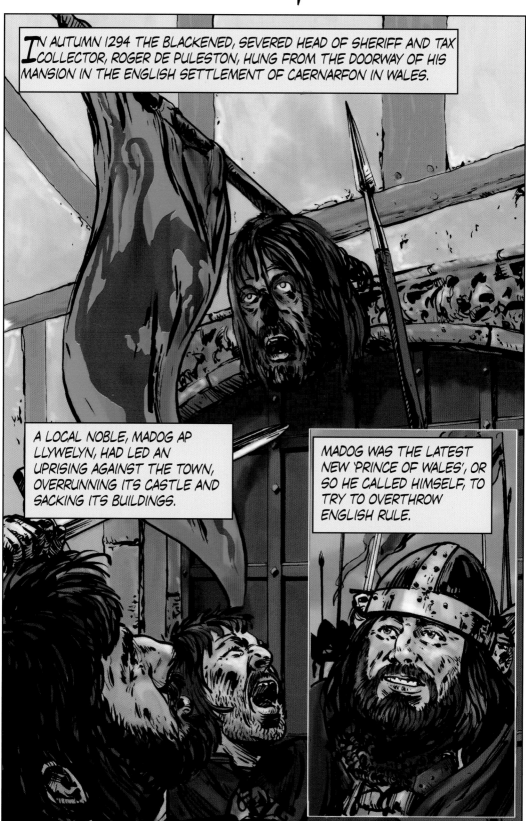

IN AUTUMN 1294 THE BLACKENED, SEVERED HEAD OF SHERIFF AND TAX COLLECTOR, ROGER DE PULESTON, HUNG FROM THE DOORWAY OF HIS MANSION IN THE ENGLISH SETTLEMENT OF CAERNARFON IN WALES.

A LOCAL NOBLE, MADOG AP LLYWELYN, HAD LED AN UPRISING AGAINST THE TOWN, OVERRUNNING ITS CASTLE AND SACKING ITS BUILDINGS.

MADOG WAS THE LATEST NEW 'PRINCE OF WALES', OR SO HE CALLED HIMSELF, TO TRY TO OVERTHROW ENGLISH RULE.

IN JANUARY 1295 ENGLISH KING EDWARD I AND AN ADVANCE PARTY OF KNIGHTS VIEWED THE RUINS OF CAERNARFON CASTLE FROM A DISTANCE.

HERE WE ARE AGAIN...

EIGHTEEN YEARS EARLIER, EDWARD HAD LED A FULL-SCALE INVASION WHEN LLYWELYN AP GRUFFYDD, THE FIRST RECOGNISED PRINCE OF WALES, HAD REFUSED TO PAY HOMAGE TO EDWARD, OR TO PAY HIS DEBTS.

THE WELSH TERRAIN HAD BEEN AS MUCH AN ENEMY AS LLYWELYN AP GRUFFYDD.

...BUT I WILL TAME THIS WILD LAND WITH NEW AND BETTER CASTLES.

ADVANCING CAUTIOUSLY, RICHARD HAD ORDERED VAST DITCHES BUILT AND THEN TIMBER FORTIFICATIONS, TO BE REBUILT LATER IN STONE.

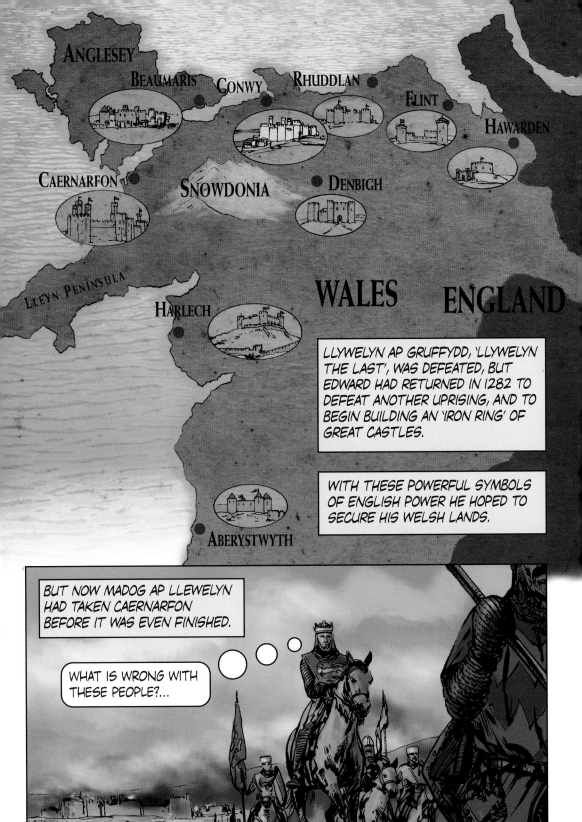

ANGLESEY

BEAUMARIS CONWY RHUDDLAN

FLINT

HAWARDEN

CAERNARFON SNOWDONIA DENBIGH

LLEYN PENINSULA

HARLECH

WALES ENGLAND

LLYWELYN AP GRUFFYDD, 'LLYWELYN THE LAST', WAS DEFEATED, BUT EDWARD HAD RETURNED IN 1282 TO DEFEAT ANOTHER UPRISING, AND TO BEGIN BUILDING AN 'IRON RING' OF GREAT CASTLES.

WITH THESE POWERFUL SYMBOLS OF ENGLISH POWER HE HOPED TO SECURE HIS WELSH LANDS.

ABERYSTWYTH

BUT NOW MADOG AP LLEWELYN HAD TAKEN CAERNARFON BEFORE IT WAS EVEN FINISHED.

WHAT IS WRONG WITH THESE PEOPLE?...

...WHY WILL THEY NOT ACCEPT MY RULE?

AS EDWARD ADVANCED DOWN THE LLEYN PENINSULA HE WAS BEING WATCHED.

AT NEFYN THEY STRUCK.

RAAAAAAAAGH!

REBELS!

ATTACKING THE BAGGAGE TRAIN, THEY CARRIED AWAY ALL OF EDWARD'S SUPPLIES.

HA HARRR!

OUT IN HOSTILE COUNTRY WITHOUT SUPPLIES, THE KING ORDERED AN IMMEDIATE RETREAT TO HIS STRONGHOLD, CONWY CASTLE.

NEWS CAME THAT REBELS HAD ARRIVED TO BESIEGE THE TOWN.

GET WORD TO THE REST OF THE ARMY TO MARCH AROUND TO GARRISON THE TOWN.

I WOULD SIRE, BUT THE RIVER - YOU NEED TO SEE IT.

THE RIVER'S IN FULL FLOOD. A HUGE STORM HAS LASHED THE MOUNTAINS!

YES, AND IT'S HEADING THIS WAY!

SUPPLIES RAN VERY LOW BUT...

YOUR EXCELLENCY, WE STILL HAVE ONE BARREL OF WINE LEFT FOR YOUR PERSONAL USE.

NO, NO, SHARE IT OUT. I BROUGHT US TO THIS PREDICAMENT. I SHOULD HAVE NO MORE THAN YOU.

OUTSIDE, THE FIERCEST STORM IN LIVING MEMORY RAGED AS EDWARD EKED OUT HIS WINE AND WAITED...

...KNOWING THAT WHEN THE WEATHER CALMED DOWN HE WOULD REUNITE WITH HIS ARMY AND **CRUSH** THE REBELLION.

THE END

Castles End

Edward III at the Battle of Crécy (1346).

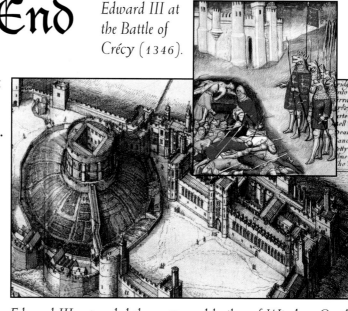

Edward I was the last English king to build so many great castles. Edward III, his grandson who reigned for 50 years, remodelled and redecorated these castles, rather than building more.

Edward III expanded the motte and bailey of Windsor Castle, using riches gained from his great victories over the French.

HIGH GOTHIC

Edward III's additions to his royal residence at Windsor pioneered a new style of architecture called Perpendicular. He built a great feasting hall with tall, elegant towers for his chivalric Knights of the Garter. By the end of the century English castles had glass windows, elaborately ornamented battlements, and fat drum towers rising from wide spurs at the base. It was 13th century-style castle-building combined with…romance.

A drum tower and spur gatehouse, Llawhaden Castle, in Wales.

English fortresses remodelled during the 14th century, such as Warwick Castle in England, were designed to be decorative rather than defensive. Building in 'castle style' reinforced the owner's lordly status.

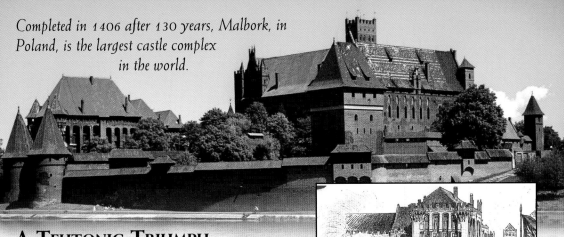

Completed in 1406 after 130 years, Malbork, in Poland, is the largest castle complex in the world.

A Teutonic Triumph

The Teutonic Knights were one of the crusading 'military orders', or warrior monks, who fought in the Holy Land. When the crusades finished they started pacifying and christianising Eastern Europe from a network of castles with Malbork, in conquered Old Prussia, as their headquarters.

Scores of small cannon were used against the walls of Malbork in 1410.

Triumphant after winning the Battle of Tannenberg, Poles and Lithuanians besieged the vast, brick-built fortress in July 1410. With great determination a tiny number of defenders resisted for two months until the attackers gave up and returned to their lands for the harvest.

Bamburgh Castle in Northumberland, England, became the first English castle to be defeated by artillery in 1464. During the War of the Roses its walls were blasted open by three cannons.

Castles Ruined

Europe has thousands of castle ruins (over 600 in the UK alone), and Britain's might have survived in much better condition had it not been for the Civil War of 1642–1651, when so many were damaged beyond repair.

Medieval bombards (cannon) became bigger and more effective at demolishing fortified walls. They signalled the end of large-scale castle building.

Glossary

Anglo-Normans Normans who lived in England after the Norman conquest of 1066.

assailed Made a concerted or violent attack upon a person or place.

bailey The outer wall of a castle.

barbican The outer defence of a castle or walled city.

besiege Surround a place with armed forces either to capture it or to force its people to surrender.

breach A gap in the fortifications or line of defence of an enemy, created by the bombardment of attacking forces.

cat A protective canopy wheeled to the base of a fortification. Also called a tortoise.

catapults A military machine worked by a lever and ropes for hurling large stones or other missiles.

depose Overthrow and remove from a position of power.

faggots A bundle of sticks, bound together to be used as fuel.

fortifications The defensive wall or other reinforcement, built to strengthen a place against attack.

Frankish Empire The large territory in today's Europe that was held by the Franks in the early Middle Ages.

The massive walls and keep of Dover Castle were completed by Henry II in 1188. The king was keen to stamp his authority on the area guarding the shortest sea crossing to France.

garderobe The toilet in a medieval building.

garrison The group of soldiers stationed in a fort or town in order to defend it.

incandescent Emitting light as a result of being heated.

keep The strongest part or central tower of a medieval castle.

lordship The territory controlled by a lord.

moat A deep, wide ditch surrounding a castle or fort, usually filled with water, built as a defence against attack.

pacifying Quelling the anger, agitation or excitement of something.

principalities States ruled by princes.

prone Likely to be affected by; vulnerable to.

quarried Extracted stone or other materials from a quarry.

realm Kingdom.

sappers Soldiers responsible for tasks such as building and repairing roads and bridges, or digging tunnels under defences.

stronghold A place that has been fortified to protect it against attack.

trebuchet A machine used in medieval siege warfare for hurling large stones or other missiles.

tumultuous Loud, noisy, deafening.

velocity Speed.

The fairytale-like Bodiam Castle in East Sussex, England, was begun in 1385 and restored in the 20th century after being severely damaged in the English Civil War.

Index